Hike in the Woods

By Erin Abriz

Illlustrated by Cheryl Kirk Noll

Jimmy pulled his sweater over his head. He looked for his cap. He had misplaced it last night. Jimmy found it under his bed.

At last, he was dressed and ready to go. He ran to get Mom. Every weekend, they went for a hike in the woods. Jimmy liked hiking, and Mom seemed to enjoy it too.

Mom knows a lot about the plants and animals. On their hikes, Jimmy would point to trees. Mom would name them. "That's an oak. This is a maple."

This morning, the cloudless sky was bright blue. "It's a perfect day," Jimmy said.

Mom put on her sunglasses to block out the brightness. Then Jimmy picked a trail. They began to follow it.

At the brook, Jimmy took off his boots and socks. He climbed on a rock on the shore. He slipped a little and began to slide. Jimmy grabbed for Mom. "Help!" he shouted.

Mom quickly helped him regain his footing. Jimmy didn't end up in the water, but his cap did.

Jimmy looked unhappy, but Mom came to the rescue again. She used a stick to pull the cap out of the brook. Jimmy wrapped it in a towel and put it in his backpack.

Then Jimmy sat down to put on his socks and boots. He saw rocks that formed a pool. In it were a few fish.

"Look, Mom! These fish are no bigger than my thumb," Jimmy exclaimed.

"Those are tadpoles, not fish," Mom said. "Tadpoles are baby frogs."

"But, Mom, frogs are tailless," Jimmy said. "These tadpoles have long tails, and they are legless. Frogs have legs."

"True, Jimmy," said Mom. "Tadpoles do not look like frogs. But they grow and change. See these tadpoles. They are getting legs."

"As tadpoles grow, their tails get shorter and shorter. They grow legs. Soon, they can spend time on land and in water."

"Ribbit! Ribbit!"

Jimmy stood still. "What was that?" he asked.

"A frog," said Mom. "Listen. Maybe we can locate it."

"Ribbit! Ribbit!"

"See it, Mom! It's on that log. It's a big one. Look at it flick at the gnats."

"Yes, it is eating the gnats. Frogs eat insects," Mom noted.

"Yuck! I'm glad I'm not a frog," Jimmy exclaimed.

"I'm glad you are not a frog too. I wouldn't like cooking bugs for your dinner," she laughed. "Speaking of eating, it's time that we get home and make lunch."

"Ribbit! Ribbit!" Jimmy laughed, and so did Mom.